Mel Bay Presents

THE VIOLINIST'S GUIDE TO

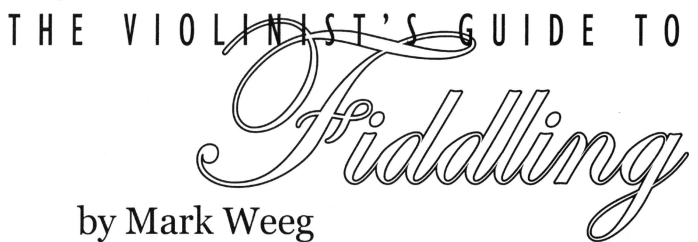

Fiddling

by Mark Weeg

D1708308

Front cover photo by Mark Weeg.

1 2 3 4 5 6 7 8 9 0

Visit us on the Web at www.melbay.com — E-mail us at email@melbay.com

TABLE OF CONTENTS

Fiddle Tunes

TABLE OF CONTENTS

ALPHABETICAL LISTING

INTRODUCTION

This book is meant for classical violinists and advanced fiddlers. I have spent more than twenty years seeking out the more difficult fiddle tunes and transcribing them as I learned them. I have collected these tunes from tapes, records, movies, television shows, and other players. There are some great fiddle tunes available in other books, but since these are available elsewhere, I do not include them herein.

This book can be used by anyone who really knows the basics of violin playing. Some of these initial instructions, however, are for the classical violinists. (You fiddlers wanting to expand your repertoire, you might want to skip ahead to the tunes. There are some things to show the classical violinists first.)

PHILOSOPHY

No one can "teach" another person to play violin (fiddle). A good "teacher" can lead the willing learner towards the right path, but it is the student who must teach himself/herself. The most the "teacher" can do is share his/her experiences (as these pertain to playing the violin) with the student.

When two fiddlers meet, and the tunes each one knows are different, a much better result will be obtained if one of the two can play chords and improvise along with the unfamiliar tunes. Aim toward this goal, and keep in mind the importance of being able to play good "second fiddle."

GENERAL NOTES

Many classically-trained violinists may find it difficult to break into a "bluegrass" style of fiddle playing. I think that there are two main reasons for this:

The first reason is that memorization is generally not stressed in the classical approach to violin playing. This is logical, since classical pieces are very long and there are so many of them - - the second reason is that strict bowing rules are learned by the classical violinists, and these strict rules are not enforced among fiddlers.

FORM

Fiddle tunes are nearly always formed in eight-measure sections. Most fiddle tunes have two lines, generally called "Line A" and "Line B." These two lines are played thus: A-A-B-B, A-A-B-B, et cetera. The tune may stop whenever the players desire, but nearly always it will stop at the end of line B, after its second time through.

Memorizing sixteen measures and the form A-A-B-B should pose no problem to any violinist who has progressed this far. As far as the bowing is concerned, relaxation of style is important, yet every effort should generally be made to start each measure with a down-bow.

FROM CLASSICAL VIOLINIST TO FIDDLE PLAYER

There are a few basics that are essential to the violinist who wants to learn to fiddle. The first thing is that speed and sonority are more important than perfection of bowing technique, within reasonable limits. Of course, speed is important in bluegrass music, but it is not the only aspect to fiddling. Fluidity of sound is essential to smooth playing, and a relaxed bowing arm is a great help to the fiddler.

BOWING

You will note that there are very few bowing marks in this book; this is because the bowing is pretty much left up to the individual player. Those that are included are felt to be fairly important, but you should feel free to bow any way that is comfortable for you.

There are some bowing details peculiar to fiddling that should be covered before we get to the tunes. The first topic to cover is what is known as "shuffling." There are two linear types of "shuffles," and three chord types, with their variations.

Apply the two linear types of bowing patterns to all of the tunes in this book. The importance of these first two patterns cannot be emphasized enough, as this is a primary difference between a classical and a bluegrass sound. The chord patterns which follow later are to be used when playing backup fiddle.

DOTTED AND FLAGGED RHYTHMS

In the interest of clarity and readability, some of the tunes which should have dots and flags throughout are just written straight. When this occurs in this book, as it does in a few places, there will be a note to you to indicate that playing a particular tune with a dotted and flagged rhythm is desirable.

   should be played

LINEAR PATTERN NO. 1
(the "single shuffle")

This is basically a (DOWN-up-down, UP-down-up) bowing pattern used to facilitate speed when playing a string of running single notes, as found in many fiddle tunes. Everybody will recognize this very common pattern. Try this "single shuffle" with the first line of "Blackberry Blossoms," as illustrated here.

This pattern is a slightly different form of the "single shuffle" that will give your playing a bluegrass feel. It requires more practice and greater accuracy because it does not involve a down-bow at the beginning of each measure. Using this pattern is most important in changing to a bluegrass sound.

I find this pattern very useful. Learn this bowing pattern by practicing it with "Durham's Reel" or "Blackberry Blossoms." The off-beats are stressed by this exercise. Mastering this pattern is essential, though at first it will make easy fiddle tunes quite challenging.

CHORD PATTERN NO.1

(the "double shuffle")

The "double shuffle" (also called the "Nashville shuffle") is used for playing backup fiddle. It is also used when kicking off a fiddle tune, especially in a group setting. It is a sort of an introduction and as such performs three functions:

1. It states the key,
2. It sets the speed, and
3. It helps all of the players start the tune at the same time, in the same place.

The pattern above shows the typical "eight potatoes" which a fiddler will generally use to lead into a fiddle tune. Note that the basic bowing pattern is the same as the "single shuffle" (L-O-N-G-short-short, L-O-N-G-short-short) but that it is being played on double strings.

This pattern is very useful when playing behind other players, and particularly singers. A healthy knowledge of chords (and perhaps the ability to read a guitarist's hands) will always serve you well when you plan to play backup fiddle.

CHORD PATTERN NO.2

(the "triple shuffle")

This is the pattern made famous by Ervin T. Rouse in his violinistic masterpiece "The Orange Blossom Special." It is essential that the violinist becomes fluent with this pattern, but also essential that he/she uses it very sparingly (except when playing Orange Blossom Special, of course). What we have here is a chord with five extra notes sprinkled above in each two-measure sequence. Generally, these five notes follow the up-and-down pattern, but those notes are left to the discretion of the individual player.

Analyze this pattern -- five triplets and one extra up-bow on the low two strings -- all sixteen beats bowed separately. Listen to "In the Mood" from the Big Band Era and note the similarities between this pattern and that tune. This might have been the origin of this bowing pattern.

Here is an eight-measure pattern to practice repetitively to help develop speed and skill with the "triple shuffle." Practice slowly at first. Work on skill and accuracy before speed. Experiment with other sets of five notes and other chord patterns. Chromatic runs can also be used with these five notes.

Practice this slowly, and progress to faster speeds only when you have it solidly under control. Measure 8 can be replaced with measure 2 if you wish.

Consider the amount of time necessary to make this pattern come as second-nature to you, and give it that time. It must become spontaneous and you must be able to deliver it smoothly and at the drop of a hat.

Vary your practice. Try this on just two strings (see the Mason's Apron variation), use different chords, change positions and use the "higher" string with a lower note on it.

(I have categorized these patterns as I have heard people refer to them, but most fiddlers simply call this pattern "shuffling.")

CHORD PATTERN NO.3
(variation of the "triple shuffle")

This is an easier way to shuffle. It is advisable, however, to become proficient with the previous "triple shuffle" pattern before learning this pattern.

What follows is an eight-measure exercise which will help you to become proficient with this altered triple shuffle pattern.

BACKUP FIDDLE PLAYING

Now it's time to play with others. You will find that many people want to sing and play, not just to listen to violinistic variations. What you will have to do is play your violin in an accompanimental fashion.

There are several ways to do this. You could play the melody along with the singers, but most singers dislike this. You could play a harmony along with the singer, but some singers may be confused by this; nonetheless, this is one of the better methods.

Knowledge of chords is essential, and the ability to read the guitar player's hands is helpful. You could play chords behind the singer, but you will have to do something with the chords.

9

"Double-shuffling" the double-stops is okay lots of times. Or you could play triple-stops on the offbeats -- this is a very good plan -- some songs require that the fiddler does just this and nothing else.

Simply "triple shuffling" (especially using the shuffles above and below) quietly in the background is another good plan. The triple shuffle can get too repetitive and sound too busy for some people with whom you may be playing, so use the "triple shuffle" sparingly at first.

Playing backup well involves many different types of accompaniment. We will next cover what I have found to be an excellent pattern.

CHORD PATTERN NO.4

(the "Corelli shuffle")

(No, not the Curly Shuffle.) This style of triple-stop playing is useful in a lot of settings, and I find it works particularly well with Cajun music. I found the basic bowing pattern in Arcangelo Corelli's Violin Sonata VI, and discovered it works well in almost all instances (except waltzes and jigs).

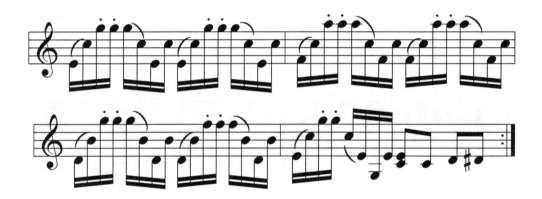

This is an easy pattern which you can always fall back on, and works well with singers. Lighten up the bow pressure and use longer bows.

CHORD PATTERN NO.5

(variation of the "Corelli shuffle")

This is the most important pattern to learn. It embodies a walking bass line, variable high notes, full-chords, and a smooth texture. This example is written here in the key of E, but it is the idea which is important. Transpose this onto the lower three strings too.

One more example of this pattern falls well under the hand in the key of D Major:

BIRLING

This trick is from Scottish fiddlers and I believe the word "birling" comes from the Scottish word for "boiling." This is admittedly a gimmick, but it can be used in very many places, as you will see throughout this book. If the triplet is not slurred, then this is probably what is intended.

This feat is accomplished with a controlled shake of your right wrist while bowing a down bow. This has the effect of giving you a very fast triplet consisting of three of the same notes or three different notes. Now, this may look easy on paper, but the effect cannot be achieved on demand without a great deal of practice. And even then, unless you hear it, it may be difficult to tell if you are doing it properly.

If you are having difficulty with this, try loosening your grip on the bow, even to the point of holding the bow with three (or even two) fingers. It's very hard to explain, so good luck. The operative thought should be one of "throwing" the bow. This is a very effective trick, though, and well worth the time you may spend on it.

Practice this at a medium speed, listening to the metronome to make sure that you don't "cheat" the surrounding notes of their time values.

TRILLS

One final note to prospective fiddlers regards the trill as used by Scottish and Irish fiddlers. Whenever possible, the trill is to be played using a note a third above the written note as the ornamental note.

CHORD PROGRESSIONS

With most of the fiddle tunes in this book I have included accompaniment chords. The student is strongly urged to find an accompanist and work with him/her as progress is made.

Another option is to play these chords yourself and record the accompaniment on tape, then play the melody along with the playback of the chords. It would be helpful to use a different instrument for this, but recording the backup with the violin will work satisfactorily.

HELPING YOUR ACCOMPANIST

These chords can be set in a measure-like format, as I do for my accompanists, as follows:

> ## Carnie's Canter
>
> F / F /Gm / Gm /F /F /Gm /C7 //
> F /F /Gm /Gm /F /F /Gm /C7 F //

(The double line at the end of each series signifies a repeat sign.)

A FEW LAST WORDS

Keep in mind that when you are a backup instrument you should probably stick to the lower three strings. Almost always, playing the low three strings is best when accompanying others. Singers will always leave a little space in their lines, generally around chord changes, into which you may place a few well-chosen notes.

With these sorts of accompaniment and your use of the bowing patterns illustrated above, other people won't feel as if their notes are being stepped on, especially if you keep it subliminal.

Good luck, and welcome to the world of fiddling. If you assiduously apply yourself to the techniques in this book, and if you play with good rhythm and intonation, I positively guarantee you a trophy or ribbon at your first fiddle contest. After all, that is the real goal of this book.

Star of County Down

This is an Irish air that I learned from some old Irish gentlemen at the "Friendship Tavern" in Rochester, New York. Every fourth Friday you could (and probably still can) find this group of Irishmen playing traditional Irish music and drinking till closing time. I learned a lot from them and none of us ever had to pay for a beer as long as there was any audience left.

When you are playing the harmony part, the F natural in the first measure should be accentuated (*ff*), as it is the indicator of the chord change. The C natural which begins the harmony's B line should also be treated the same. Except for these two spots, stay at a volume level generally just a bit lower than the person playing the actual melody.

TUNES

BLUEGRASS FIDDLE TUNES

Arkansas Traveller

What we have here is a very common American fiddle tune. David Bromberg played this on an album, calling it "The Boggy Road to Milledgeville." That's when I quit playing guitar and started playing violin.

The variation has a bluegrass-style B line which I heard on the PBS TV show in New York, called "Bluegrass Ramble."Whenever a fiddler would come on screen during that program, I would turn on my tape recorder. Whatever was played that evening was my lesson for the month, as this was only a monthly TV program.

That B line is fun to play, and I thought that this yokel had come up with it. I learned it nonetheless. A few years later I heard somebody famous on the radio -- I still don't know who that was -- and he was playing this same B line note for note. That "yokel" on the local TV station must have learned it from that same recording.

Bodie McCaffrey

Written by myself back in Rochester and named for my girlfriend at the time. The G Major scale with the E note stressed lends a kind of bluegrass feel.

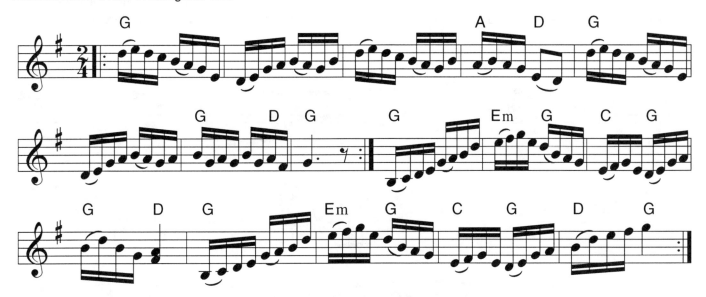

Blackberry Blossoms

This is a very popular and well-known fiddle tune among bluegrass, old-timey, and Irish players. I have taken the final section of Hayden's Symphony #88 in G Major, second violin part, changed it just slightly so that it fits the form, and used it as the variation of the A line. This variation is also a good high harmony to play while some other instrumentalist is playing the straight melody line.

As regards high harmonies, these must be played with greater tact than lower harmonies. Maintain good eye contact with the melody person, and be polite.

Drunken Billy Goat

Another bluegrass fiddle tune picked up from the bluegrass radio program in Denver. Many other fiddlers must have heard this also, because the next summer at fiddle contests all around town I heard this tune played.

Durham's Reel

This bluegrass fiddle tune has a different form than usual. This one is always played in the form A-A-B-A. You will find that there are a few other bluegrass tunes played with this form, but remember that this is an exception, not the rule.

I learned the straight version from one of my few fiddle teachers. The variation was picked off of the radio in Rochester. At the time I didn't even know the name of the tune, but I luckily had my tape recorder turned on. I heard a version very close to this played at a Colorado bluegrass festival.

Make sure that the high E harmonic really screams, and slide it clearly back down to first position.

Red Wing

This fiddle tune comes from a folk song about a "Union Maid." Or maybe the song was written to go along with the pre-existing melody. Repeats are not used in this tune because each line states its theme twice already.

In the first variation are some classically-oriented sequences. Line B ends with a G major scale with the extra G♯. This is good to use any time the tune is played, whether you are doing the straight melody, a variation, or playing backup chords for others. You can also use this ending with any tune in this key, or you can put it into other keys and use it for endings of other fiddle tunes.

I have included one extra A line here; use it as another variation when the tune gets played more than twice.

Red Wing (continued)

Three Waltzes

<u>Laura's Waltz</u>: Included with "Teenager Waltz" and "Louis' Waltz," this is most likely Irish.

<u>Louis' Waltz</u>: Don't know much about this waltz; I learned it a long time ago and I have been told that it is called "Louis' Waltz," and thus I have applied that title here.

<u>Teenager Waltz</u>: "K-Tel Productions Presents 30 Bluegrass Fiddlers" tape (I think) was where I found this waltz. Each of these waltzes could be played separately, of course.

<u>Note:</u> When you play these waltzes separately, make sure to start with the three pick-up notes from the end of the waltz which come before it in this medley.

Laura's Waltz

Louis' Waltz

Teenager Waltz

Salt Creek

This tune I learned from a banjo player who didn't bring his capo that day, so I learned it first in the key of G. Since everybody really plays it in A, that is the key I have used here.

Leading into the first B line we use what classical violinists call the flying spiccato and fiddlers call bouncing the-bow. Just make sure the bow moves along the string while it is bouncing.

All the open-string pizzicati are to be played with the left hand. The D note on the fourth line of the staff is to be plucked with the right hand, so make sure you lead up to it with an up-bow.

In the B line of the variation, a glissando up to the A note with the index finger is encouraged. This will place you in third position for the C♯, from whence you should slide back down to the open E string.

CAJUN TUNES

A Cajun Fiddle Tune

Strong double stops, a strong beat, and simple chords mark this tune, which is pretty typical for the genre. I heard it on the radio up in New York, and include it here to increase your repertoire of double-string fiddle tunes. Play this with full double-stops, generally the higher open string.

23

Up Jumped the Devil

This tune comes from Ralph's Top Shop, a bluegrass meeting place in Denver, and I have given this one enough of a Cajun sound to justify its being placed in this section. Some people think of this as a bluegrass piece, but not me.

Diggy Liggi Li

This is the ever-popular Cajun song about a Diggi Liggi Li (boy) finding his Diggy Liggy Lo (girl). Very touching, very flashy. The little open notes sprinkled throughout the tune are indicative of string (and/or stopped notes) to be played along with the written notes. Thus, this is to be played with full double stops.

Jolie Blonde

As I see it, there are two styles of Cajun tunes. The first type is the Hollywood-ized glamorized simple American country style, as the other Cajun tunes here exemplify. The other type is the more ubiquitous simplistic waltzes and dance tunes which are more truly authentic. This tune is one of the latter, and is often requested by people who may not be familiar with it, just with its title. They may not be happy with the tune once you play it. It has been my experience that the mainstream American public likes the other sort more.

26

CLASSICAL FIDDLE TUNES
Carnival of Venice

During my classical training days I encountered a few different composers who each included variations of this famous tune and their own "moto perpetuo." Thus I think it appropriate that I include my own variations which I wrote in 1987 (I figured my variations would be easier to play than Paganini's variations.).

I actually wrote this out to play on viola as my audition with a local community orchestra. I got the principal viola position with it.

CARNIVAL OF VENICE

VARIATION I

VARIATION II

Carnival of Venice (continued)

VARIATION IV

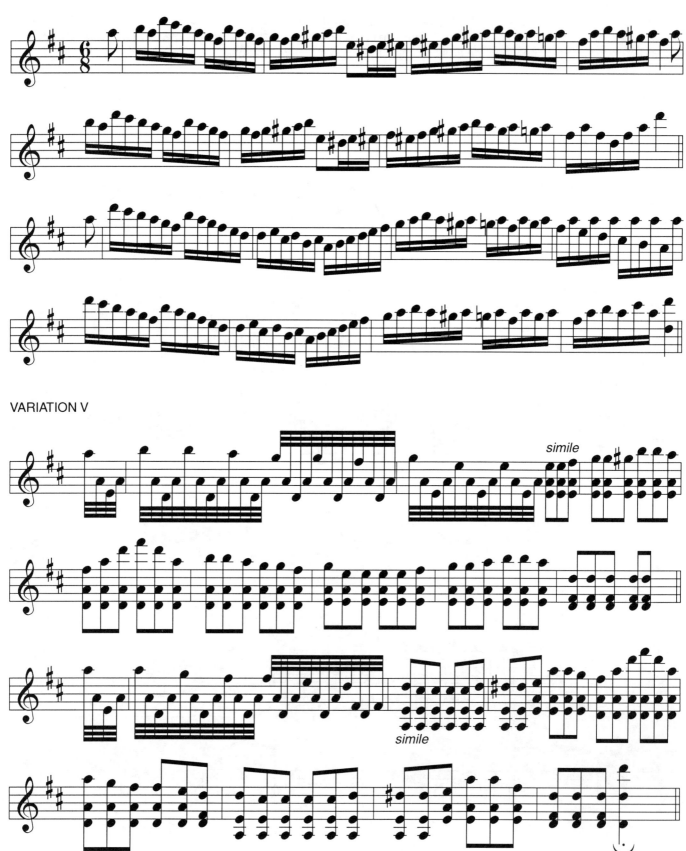

VARIATION V

Zigeunerweisen

First off, though I dislike apologizing in advance, I apologize to all of the classical violinists who play this piece. It is a travesty to take such a magnificent piece of music and simplify it as I have done here. Nonetheless, this is the only way it can be brought to a playable level for most people (i.e. myself).

When you get to the A Major section the first time, wrap up that previous A minor section dramatically, and then start out slowly with the A Major part. Pick up speed rapidly in the very first measure, until you have regained the original tempo. The bow should bounce slightly to make these notes stand out (in the A Major and D Major sections).

Zigeunerweisen (continued)

COUNTRY/AMERICAN FIDDLE TUNES
Alvin Yardley Tune

Recorded by the Arkansas Sheiks, this was my first lesson in transcribing difficult tunes. My girlfriend at that time helped me out by transcribing the first line. When I asked her to keep going and do the second line, she said that I had to figure that line out. A tough lesson at the time, but it is better if one transcribes the tunes oneself.

On the record they said that Alvin Yardley did not write this tune, but that it was written to match the style in which he played. Apparently, this Alvin Yardley guy was a pretty famous Texas swing fiddler in his day. This should have a very swingy ragtime feel.

Banks of the Ohio

An old hillbilly song about a man who kills his intended lover. When people sing this, it is sung rather slowly. Thus, control of the bow is very important, as I find it easy to get carried away with the speed. The variations, both low and high, are sort of Cajun-sounding when it is played fast. Played slow, it just sounds complicated and mournful.

32

Clarinet Polka

I learned this tune in E♭ and then I had asked around and found that when fiddlers play this, they play it in the key of G. Thus, when I transposed it from the key of E♭, I naturally chose G.

The form for this tune should be A-A-B-B-A-A-C-C-A.

Demonstration Rag

Garrett Sullivan, a banjo-playing doctor friend of mine gave me a tape loaded with banjo solos. This was the only one they played slow enough and melodic enough to figure out. Note that the last line of the B section is just the first half raised up an octave (mostly).

34

Jessie Polka

I heard this tune when I went to watch Ron Jones play. The next day I cornered him and asked him to play it for my tape recorder. He graciously played it three times in succession for me, and I include here exactly as he played it.

Keep in mind that the form in which it was played was as follows: intro-A-A-B-B-A-C-C-D-D-E-B-B-A.

John Reading's Graduation Reel

Written by me as a graduation gift for John Reading, a gifted pianist and a person very tolerant of fiddlers, most likely because his wife Sue plays fiddle with their band.

Maple Leaf Rag

Transcribed and key-changed directly from the piano score, this was originally written out by me to be played by solo mandolin. I have subsequently found that with careful fingering in the various positions it is possible to play on violin, and as this book is meant for the classical violinist, you might have the ability to play the triple stops in these positions, too. So have at it.

On violin I play a lot of double stops where the triple stops (so easy on a mandolin) should be. This is one of Scott Joplin's best rags, and I have not simplified it at all. If you have a mandolin, that might be a better place to start with this one.

Nowadays I have taken to playing the following two measures in place of measures 7 and 8:

Maple Leaf Rag

Scott Joplin

Maple Leaf Rag (continued)

38

Country-Style Hoedown

This is a chord progression I put together to introduce a violin-playing friend to the style of country fiddling. I figure I probably ought to put words to this, but in advance of that, I include it here to familiarize you with some rather typical country chord changes.

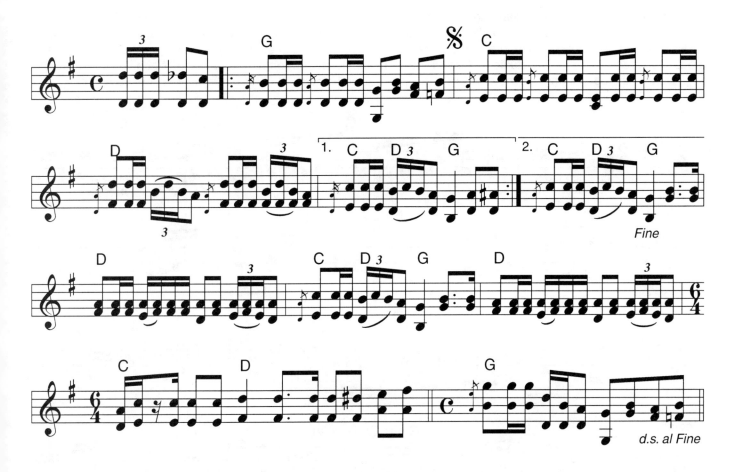

Whiskey Before Breakfast

This tune is so commonly played that I include it in the American fiddle tunes section. I have found there is a French Canadian version (the variation) to go with the traditional Irish tune. I learned the Irish version in the Golden Link Country Dance Orchestra in Rochester, and the French-Canadian version from a Clem Myers record.

I spent a whole summer learning nearly every last note on that Clem Myers record, and I would advise you to find a recording of a good fiddler who plays standard fiddle tunes, and try your best to learn to "learn by ear." It's better to use a record that was recorded in a studio, rather than in live performance for this ear-training exercise. Tape speeds are under stricter control in the studio and thus re-tuning your violin between cuts is obviated. When you do this eartraining, listen for the open strings as the tune passes by; these can help you to determine what key the piece is in.

Wildwood Flower

This is an old Carter Family song, and it was originally written as it is here. Nowadays, however, some singers do not pause so long between the lines, so the noodling around on the A Major chord between the phrases may have to be cut down, depending on with whom you play this.

FRENCH CANADIAN FIDDLE TUNES
Blackberry Quadrille

I've heard this called by other names a long time ago; it is a very old tune. Another version going around has a simpler chord progression at the end of the B line (no C chord). I like to play it as it is here, with more of a polka-like ending.

Cregthorne Schottische

I have been told this is called "Craig Thorne's Schottische," but I am not really sure of that. Note the diminished chord at the end of the third line; that's what makes this one unique. Not too fast, now.

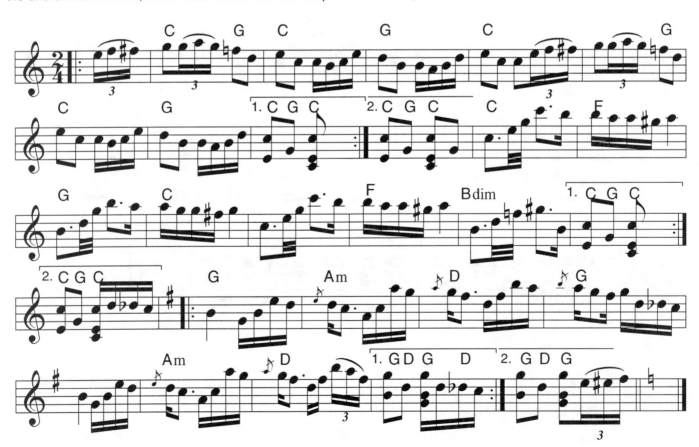

Hal Casey Medley
LIL BURNT POTATO

A French-Canadian jig, included because Hal Casey kicked off this medley with it when I heard this on the Bluegrass Ramble TV show.

SNOWFLAKE REEL

The B♭ chord mades this piece well worth the time spent. Note the use of the triple shuffle in an otherwise ordinary fiddle tune.

The measure just before the B♭ chord in the second line can also be played, as I currently do, thusly:

And as long as we're at it, this pattern can come up again nearer the end, in the second-to-last measure, to be played thusly:

JOYS OF QUEBEC

An excellent fiddle tune, with a driving momentum all its own. Use left-hand pizzicato on the open E near the beginning of the B line.

BIG JOHN McNEILL

I remember wanting to learn this tune long before I was able to handle it. Dick Bolt, "the fiddlin' physician," did show me the first few measures, but it took a while for me to pick the rest off of my tape.

(I heard an interesting way of playing "Big John McNeill," and suggest it here: Since each line uses only three adjacent strings, the keys can be changed by switching which three strings you play on at any given time. For clarification, if this helps, play this form A-A-B-B-A-A-B-B in the keys of A-A-D-D-E-E-A-A. Just a thought.)

Snowflake

Segue

③ Joys of Quebec

④ Big John McNeill

Fine

44

Mark Weeg's Reel

This is the first tune I ever wrote, and I tried to keep it in the style of J. Scott Skinner, on whom I had been over-dosing at the time.

Upon playing it for others, the best compliment I have received is "Well, it's within the idiom."

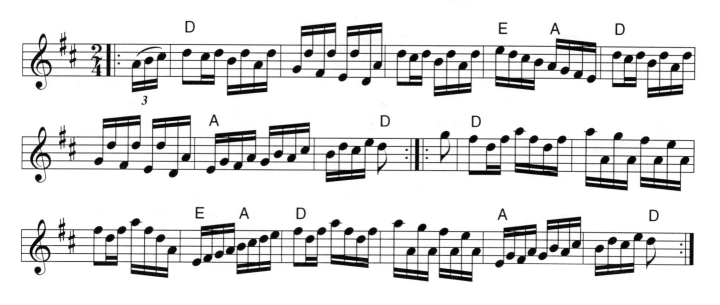

Tea Gardens

traditional

Moonlight Clog

The New One

The New One (continued)

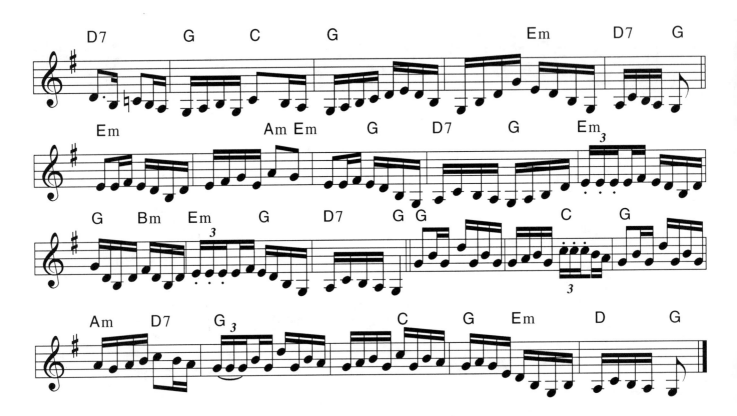

Newcastle Hornpipe

This comes from an old Scottish tape. The bowing was very clear and helped put the lilt into this hornpipe. In this book we generally have tried to leave the bowing up to the player, so let this be the exception to prove that rule.

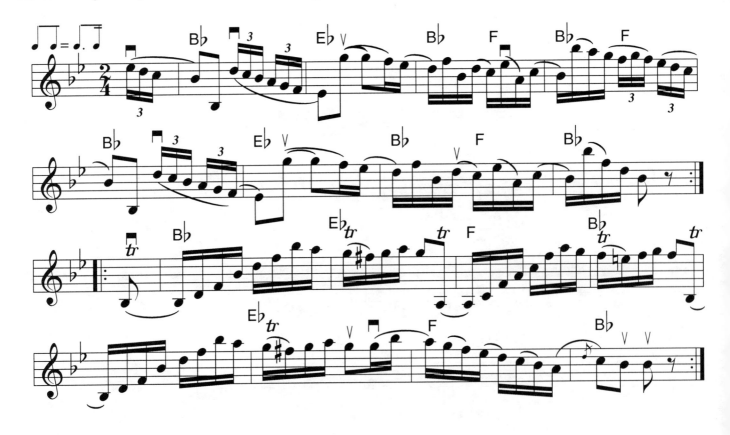

Rover's Fancy

I watched David Bromberg play this live in concert, and then learned it just as he played it. Yes, it does go into second position and then third position in the B section. There are easier ways to play this line, and if it is played all in first position it has the title "High Level Hornpipe.

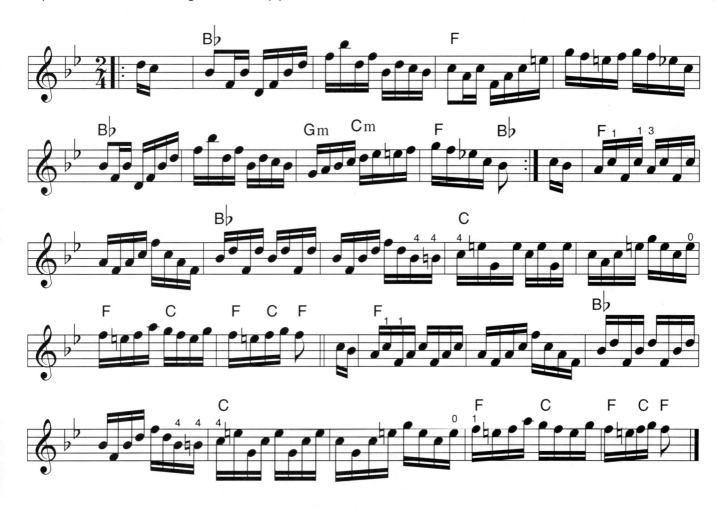

Rupert Fain's Haggis

I met Rupert Fain in New York. He was consistently friendly and positive, and I wrote this for him. He wanted me to name it after him, but he wanted me to include his nick-name "Haggis." Thus the title.

49

Amazing Grace

This is one of the old standard songs which everybody knows. The first line is in D Major, and it relies heavily on the drone of the D string. Use the 4th finger when necessary. Then we change keys, and use the G string to drone with. These are the two keys which people I have known have sung it in. Feel free to put it into other keys when you play with other singers.

The Old Rugged Cross

My father used to sing in the choir, and I could sit there and watch him sing. This song is guaranteed to bring back the old memories.

What a Friend We Have in Jesus

One more of the old standards. I have been told of a Christmas display which had little marionette shopkeepers standing outside of their little shops, singing this song.

Allen's Reel (Alan's Reel)

Tony Williams the mandolin player went on a vacation somewhere in the Southeast and taped a fiddler whom he met. On the tape this elderly gentleman calls out the name of the tune as "Allen's Reel! Allen's Reel!" in a perturbed tone of voice, and then he played it. Tony and I took to calling it by the double name right away.

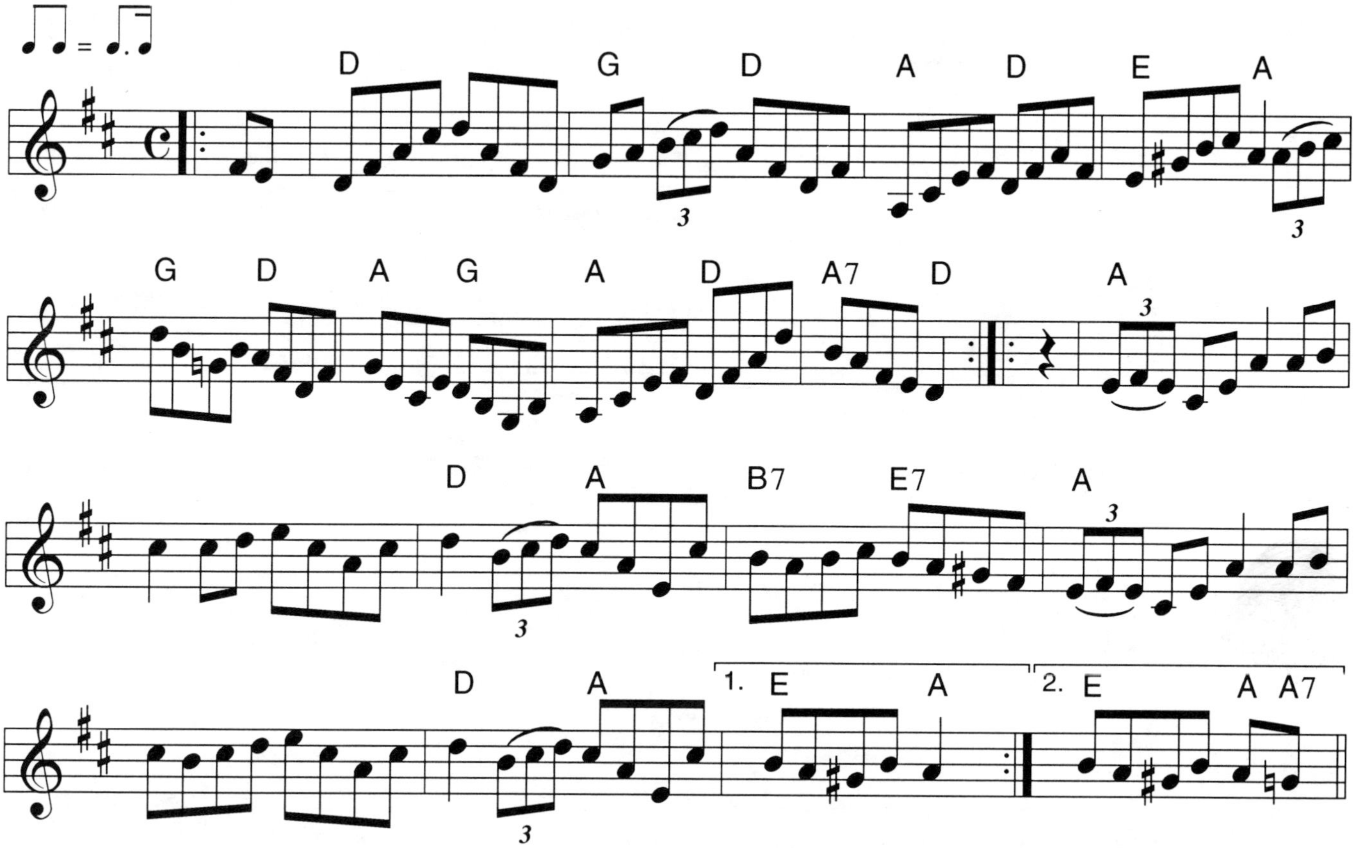

Devil's Dream

54

Harvest Home

Hornpipe with Variations
(Sean McGuire's Version)

Lord Gordon's Reel
(Michael Coleman's Version)

Mason's Apron
(Sean McGuire's Version)

Mason's Apron (continued)

Sailor's Hornpipe

This tune is often called "Popeye." It was originally a Scottish tune called "The College Hornpipe," and as such was played in B♭.

I encourage the student, whenever possible, to learn tunes in two or more keys. One never knows what key some new player may know a piece in, and it is always best to be flexible when a discrepancy crops up. When you play in a different key, your mind opens to a wider variety of possibilities for making up your own variations, not only for the current tune, but for other tunes as well.

Though this is called a hornpipe, it is most often played like a reel, without the dotted and flagged rhythm that most horpipes use.

Un Cnoc Cein Mhic Cainte

Don't ask me to pronounce the title. This Air came from a tape from one of my students, and its title is in Gaelic. No translation was available.

The chords above the music are a basic accompaniment, but since it is an Air, the fiddler should take a lot of liberty with the rhythm. I like to think of this as a four-line poem, with two phrases for each line here. These four phrases (disregarding repeats) should be played as slowly and dramatically as possible.

60

SCOTTISH FIDDLE TUNES

Arthur Seat

A great fiddle tune, named by J. Scott Skinner for a geographic landmark (a double mountain top, or "seat") in Scotland.

Banks

Written by a person named Parazotti, this is found in the Scottish repertoire nonetheless. This tune is said to be one of the hardest Scottish fiddle tunes to play, but that is probably because of the key signature.

One might try triple-shuffling through the spelled-out chords in the B line; it lends a little bit of bluegrass to the piece.

Bride's Reel

Definitely one of the faster Scottish fiddle tunes. For dramatic effect, one should take the first four notes together on an up-bow, then lift the bow off the strings after the D note. To help increase speed, set the bow down about a foot from the frog and keep it there, using only right wrist and right hand movement (no arm movements) to power through this tune at breakneck speed.

Carnie's Canter

The canter referred to here is likely the little practice pipe that bagpipers use to practice their fingering on without blowing up the whole bagpipe. This is a very intense little tune. I like to follow this up with "My brother's Letter" as the speeds are close and the key change is a very nice effect, too. Warn your accompanists to fasten their seat belts.

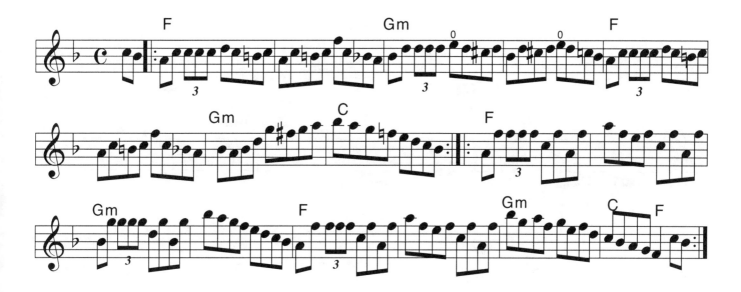

My Brother's Letter

Another tune from Ted McGraw's Christmas Tape. (see page 65 re: explanation of term) Ted told me that when I could play this tune, I would then be allowed to refer to myself as a Scottish Violinist.

Lightning speed, please.

East Neuk O'Fife

A traditional Scottish fiddle tune, set apart from all the rest by the E minor chord used to end each line. Like "Salt Creek," the accompaniment for both line A and line B is identical. This type of chord patterning is ideal when you play with accompanists who have difficulty discerning when the soloist changes from line A into line B. See the Book "The Scottish Violinist" for more and better variations; these are just the ones I wrote.

Eugene Stratton

Rather similar in character and key to "Arthur Seat," this tune was written in honor of a Vaudeville star of the day, a gentleman likely named Eugene Stratton.

One has two options in the second line, the first being to separate all the notes in the first whole measure, and the other option being to hit the high B♭ with the end of the down-bow, then slur the upcoming B♭-A-B♭ on the up-bow. You decide which you like better.

Happy Go Lucky Hornpipe

Ted McGraw, virtuoso accordionist and spiritual leader of instrumental folk music in Rochester gave me a tape for Christmas and this tape included all of the tunes which he felt I ought to know. I took his advice and learned much of that tape, the "Christmas Tape," as I labelled it.

Play this with a dotted and flagged rhythm, as it is a hornpipe.

J. Scott Skinner Medley

Clayton's Strathspey

This first tune is slow and dramatic, and should be played in a somewhat "classical" style. The high A note in the first measure of the second line could be played as a harmonic. The backward flagged notes should be played with a snap, pausing for effect.

Spring Bank House Strathspey

The second tune is off of the Ted McGraw Christmas tape. The speed should increase slightly when you start into this tune.

Bonnie Banchory

Now the speed really picks up. I learned this tune in my sleep. I decided to follow the Suzuki method and listen to this tune over and over. After a few days of this, I awoke one morning and realized I was playing this tune in my dreams. I wrote it down right away and it didn't need much changing after that.

66

J. Scott Skinner Medley (continued)

BONNIE BANCHORY *Allegro*

Lucania Polka

   In the earlier part of this century, when record companies were just forming, there were ongoing competitions all over the world to find the best players of any type of indigenous music. J. Scott Skinner was discovered then, and he was brought over to America on the ocean liner named "The Lucania." I read that he composed this polka while on board that ocean liner.

   The form is: A-B-B-A--C-D-C--A-B-B-A. Yes, the seemingly introductory D chord (note) at the beginning of line A is still included each time you play that section.

Miss Drummond of Perth's Favorite Scotch Measure

The Boulder International Folk Dancers committee gave me a tape of tunes to learn, that I might play for their first annual Haggis Ball, and this was the best of the lot. Play this one slow, if you like, and use all the double stops and ornamentation you can think of.

The form should be: A-B-B-C-C.

69

Robert Cormack

Another tune from Ted McGraw's "Christmas Tape." It should be played slowly, in a dramatic and regal style. I find this goes well when you follow it with "Happy Go Lucky Hornpipe" and then "Carnie's Canter." The speeds will increase from slow to medium to fast when you play it as such.

70

Slocklit Light
One of the better-known Shetland fiddle tunes. Play it slowly, pure and simple.
Smith O'Couster
A snappy little tune, very strophic, which goes well with the Slocklit Light. This might be a Shetland tune, but more likely it is just Scottish. The speed should increase just a bit from the speed of the first tune.
Da Grocer
A little faster than the first two, this is another tune off of one of my students' tapes.

Strathspey in E♭

Another Scottish tune picked up so far back that I don't even remember where it came from, but at least I got the title correct. Don't play this one too fast.

<u>DUETS</u>

Bach Invention XIII

Johann Sebastian Bach wrote "inventions" as lessons for his students. I have taken the right hand of the pianist, made that the first violin part, and the left hand has become the second violin part. This one did not require a key change, just octave changes.

Bach Invention #XIII in Am

Violin I

M. Weeg, Arrangement

73

Bach Invention XIII

Violin II

M. Weeg, Arrangement

Bach Invention XIV

Another of Bach's inventions, here changed from the original key of B♭. This works out particularly well in this key, but requires the second violin to pay strict attention to the timing. Once it starts rolling, it gets easier.

Violin I

M. Weeg, Arrangement

75

Bach Invention XIV

Violin II

M. Weeg, Arrangement

Badinerie

Taken from Bach's Orchestral Suite No.2 in B minor. The first violin plays the flute part, the second violin plays the music to all the string sections. I recruited John Fodor to assist me with some of the stylistic nuances, as he was my violin teacher at that time.

Violin I

M. Weeg, Arrangement

Badinerie

Violin II

M. Weeg, Arrangement

Deurmyer Trepak

Violin I

Deurmyer Trepak (continued)

Violin II

Duo Chromatique

My first violin teacher, Sister Mary Jean, didn't show up for one of our lessons, so I sat in her office and copied this duet out of one of her old books.

This piece of music can be played with minimal finger-sliding if you learn the stretch of open string A to 4th finger stretched F (still on the A string). It is a good idea to memorize this stretch anyway, as it comes in handy in a lot of chromatic runs.

Violin I

Duo Chromatique

Violin II

Jenny Lind Polka

This is an old cotillion dance tune, one of the first pieces I orchestrated for the Denver Mandolin Society, with whom I played for a long time. This will help you involve another fiddler in your playing. The melody is one of the oldest traditional American tunes, and I picked this up from some piano sheet music.

Classical violinists will recognize the form, but it may not be familiar to the fiddlers. Just take all the repeats down the page the first time, and when you hit the d.c., go back to the top and then ignore the repeats all the way down the the *Fine*.

Violin I

Jenny Lind Polka

Violin II

Sir Borman Waltz

This is a French-Canadian waltz, learned from the playing of Clem Myers. In my earliest learning days, I played constantly with John Culligan, another fiddler. I learned to improvise backup fiddle so that we would not always be playing the same thing.

Some people call this "playing second fiddle," but the true virtuoso fiddler (you) should always be able to make up a harmony for any tune someone else knows. Sometimes this beats learning someone else's tune.

The harmony part almost stands on its own; that is the goal of any variation you may write for any tune.

Sir Borman Waltz

Violin II

She's Big, She's Small

An Irish air, arguably written about two mountains. This was my first teaching experience. Twenty years ago, Jym was going to get married, and John and John and Joe were going to play for the wedding. Jym wanted this piece to be played, and Joe and the Johns came to me to transcribe it and teach it to them. This is exactly as I delivered it to them. Some improvements might be made now in the harmonies, in the light of further education, but they are still valid nonetheless.